WHEN HIP HOP
MEETS THE CHRIST

WHEN HIP HOP
MEETS THE CHRIST
Interactive Work Book/Study Guide

VOLUME 1

JOSHUA (OASIS) GRANT

XULON PRESS

Xulon Press
2301 Lucien Way #415
Maitland, FL 32751
407.339.4217
www.xulonpress.com

Printed in the United States of America.

ISBN-13: 978-1-54561-563-8

There are **3 Goals** for this **Ministry**:

- <u>GLORIFY</u> *(Reverence, Respect, & Give the HONOR to)* **GOD ALLMIGHTY FATHER MOST HIGH**

- <u>Exalt JESUS</u> **SAVIOR & LORD Over ALL**

- <u>Give People HOPE</u> (**IN JESUS**) **thru LOVE & THE HOLYSPIRIT**

This is an Interactive Workbook/Study Guide, that will cause its users to pick up a pen, a BIBLE, and use their Faith. It will include activities such as: Truth or False, Inspirational footnotes, a little multiple choice and some reading (Scriptures). Users will understand how to **battle** and **overcome** obstacles and opposition by using their **Faith in GOD**. This will develop their **Trust in GOD**. Some words such as (GOD, JESUS, HOLYSPIRIT and a few more Kingdom Words) were written in all capitalization. The author chose to write those specific words that way as giving honor to GOD and Exalting JESUS even through his writing. There is an Interactive Radio broadcast that can be used to explain the topics of this workbook in more detail. Just search the internet for "When Hip Hop Meets THE CHRIST" or go to blogtalkradio.com/O_a_ sis. This is the first volume of a continual series of workbooks, this volume lines up with episodes 1-20 of the radio broadcasts. Thanks for your purchase and support!

Table of Contents Page

Lesson 1-True Life

Personal Encouragement: Life is More than Gain in things on the earth (Matthew 6:25, Romans 5:3-4, John 16:33).

*Tribulation = Perseverance (Overcoming Power)
*Perseverance = Character
*Character = Hope

There is *a lot more* to Life than just eating food. Is not, **the body** used for *more than* just putting on clothes? Circle one: THE TRUTH or False (see Matthew 6:25)

1. <u>Genesis 1:1</u> shows the beginning of time for all humans. <u>John 1:1</u> also shows another beginning, even before time, so according to <u>John 1:1-4 & 14</u> who is this *very important person*, whom *the entire human race* Lives **depends** on?
   A. JESUS
   B. devil
   C. Michael The Arc Angel
   D. None of these

Personal Encouragement: JESUS is the Source (center) of My Faith, Joy, Worship, Praise & LOVE.

2. *Hearing* the **Preaching and Teaching of JESUS THE CHRIST** is Good News.

*Did you know that War started in HEAVEN? (Revelation 12:7-12 & Isaiah 14:12-15)

1

3. **Who** fought against the devil a nd threw him and a third of the angels out of HEAVEN?
   A. Gabriel
   B. Adam & Eve
   C. Michael and his Angels
   D. Peter

4. **THE TRUTH** *seems* to be *unbelievable* by situations, circumstances, experiences, and mindsets. *These things* can make us want to question **GOD'S LOVE** and **GOD'S JUSTICE**. When you don't *Understand* you should **TRUST in GOD** and Not panic!

Personal Encouragement: Do not Parade or put *Your Doubts* on Blast more than you put your Trust in GOD on Blast; boast in HIM and of HIM.

5. <u>Rejecting</u> **JESUS** = ETERNAL TRAGEDY

Rejecting satan + **Submitting To GOD** = **ETERNAL LIFE** (Read James 4:7-10)

Lesson 2-True Work

1. What is **Work**? Man's definition says, **work** is something produced by **Mental Effort** or **Physical Labor**, an *artistic* production (as book or needle work), material in the process of manufacture, occupation, employment, business, pursuit, calling.

    Work is also defined as, to fashion or create a *useful* or *desired* product through labor or exertion, something that has to be done (being productive with your Life), doing work or pieces of work for hire or pay.

2. **FAITH** without Works or **Action** is dead. (Read James 2:14-19)

3. It takes *a **willing** mind* to work or be productive with your life.

Personal Note: Work is Action, you being Active to produce an expected end, not just sitting there letting time and Life pass you by!

4. **GOD HIMSELF is THE CREATOR OF WORK and HE even Works.** (Read Genesis 2:2)

5. **Read** and **Meditate** on Psalm 8:3-9.

6. Which of these things did **GOD** Create???
    A. All Humans
    B. The Stars Moon and Sun

   C. Angels

   D. GOD Made All Of These.

7. Man goes out to his work and to his labor until evening, Read **Psalm 104:23**.

8. What shall we do that we may work **The Works of GOD**? (Read **John 6:28-29**)

   A. Go get a job

   B. Get a career

   C. Believe in **JESUS**

   D. Go to church

JESUS said, "I must work The Works of HIM who sent ME while it is day; the night is coming when no man can work. HE also says, "Do not labor for the food which perishes, but for The Food which endures to Everlasting Life" Read **John 6:27**.

Do not save up your *treasure on earth*, thieves can steal that and it can be destroyed. Save up your treasure in HEAVEN, thieves cannot reach it there and you will have access to it forever Read **Matthew 6:19-21**.

Personal Note: Build up Treasure in HEAVEN by *Depositing LOVE* on the earth.

Seek GOD First and HE will Add what you need in your life Read **Matthew 6:25-34**.

Lesson 3-I Am Not My Clothes

1. **THE LORD** does not see as humans see. Humans look at *the outward appearance* and judge, **BUT THE LORD** looks at *the heart* of the person (Read **1Samuel 16:7**).

2. **Physical Appearance,** clothes; suit and tie VS jeans and t-shirt, does this describe your *worth* or your *comfort*?

3. **Personal Note: GOD Desires UNITY not Uniformity.** I do not have to dress formal to come to church, I can come comfortable.

4. Those who focus on *the outward or physical* **only**, according to **Luke 11:39-40**, **THE LORD** calls this kind of mindset, which of the following???
    A. Foolish Ones
    B. Wise Ones
    C. Christians
    D. Humans

5. Do not let your adornment (beautification) be outward only, rather let it be *the hidden person of the heart*, this is Very Precious in **The Sight of GOD** according to **1Peter 3:3-4.** THE TRUTH or False

    Food For Thought: Because we are living in a society that has lost its **right** mind, it is important to dress decent and appropriately. If females dress revealing too much skin then the *immorality* of most males will be controlled by his lust instead of Love, which may cause him to be disrespectful to the female. As well as for the males, if we wear baggy clothes and a backwards hat, we run the risk of being harassed by police, being labled a thief or thug up to no good, or even possibly being shot and killed. You can wear what you want but unfortunately the society we live in labels you by your clothes, but do not let them. We must be careful and conscience that others may see you differently and may even misinterpret what you are saying thru the expression of your clothes.

*Do not Love the world or the things of the world (world mentality). If anyone loves the world, **THE LOVE OF THE FATHER** is **not** in them. For all that is in the world- **the lust** of the flesh, **the lust** of the eyes and **the pride** of life- is **not** of **THE FATHER** but is of the world. And *the world is passing away*, and the lust of it, but they who **do THE WILL OF GOD** will abide forever 1John 2:15-17.

All that is in the world is lust, more lust and pride. All these are against the way that FATHER Created us and that's why *the lust*, *the world*, and *its pride* is passing away daily!

Lesson 4-Religion Vs Relationship with THE CREATOR

Religion
Good Behavior
My Own Righteousness
Distant from GOD
Know THE CREATOR as GOD Only **not** as FATHER
Don't Know JESUS,
Don't Honor THE CHRIST of GOD

Relationship
LOVE & FORGIVENESS
GRACE & MERCY
HIS WAY/ THE TRUTH
Close to GOD
Know THE CREATOR as GOD and FATHER
Accepts & Honors **JESUS THE CHRIST** as **LORD**

1. THE TRUTH or False: According to **Isaiah 64:6** *our own righteousness* is compared to Filthy Rags.

2. Read and Meditate on these two verses (Romans 10:3 & Philippians 3:9) *Now You choose: **GOD'S Righteousness which is FAITH in JESUS** or your own Righteousness which is keeping the law (behaving good enough).

Religion- the service and worship of GOD, according to **human** dictionary definition.

But according to **THE WORD OF GOD**, pure and unde-filed religion before GOD and THE FATHER is this, to *visit orphans and widows in their trouble and to keep one's self unspotted from the world* (**James 1:27**).

GOD *seeks* and *wants* a **Relationship** with HIS human race, HE'S not seeking religion as we know it and think THE TRUTH or False? (**Read John 1:1-4**).

JESUS did not die to give us religions, but HE died and GOD Resurrected HIM to give us a Loving Relationship with GOD our FATHER; this is Life. (Read John 1:14)

Lesson 5-Sex, Sex, and More Sex

GOD Created Sex! Before **GOD** told us "Thou shall not," HE told us to "Be Fruitful and Multiply". **HIS PURPOSE** for sex is **Pure**, it is for Reproduction, for Closeness, and for Pleasure between a man and his wife.

Sex becomes *perverted* when we take it out of *the context* that **GOD** put it in. We think and the media influences us to think that sex is just for pleasure, leaving out its purity, reproduction, and closeness (Intimacy). Read 1 John 2:15-17

1. 1. Which of these choices is the **most important** and is **Everlasting**?
   A. Lust
   B. Love
   C. Money
   D. None of these

Did you know:

¤ King David was the Godliest man on earth, had a heart after **GOD**, but got caught up in his lust for another man's wife. He then had her husband killed so that he could have her as his wife. (Adultery and Murder)

¤ Samson Loved **THE LORD**, talked to HIM and Obeyed HIM, but his lust for the woman Delilah made him go against **the command of GOD** and he revealed his secret to her.

- <u>King Solomon</u> (King David's son), wrote Proverbs, Ecclesiastes, & Song of Solomon in THE BIBLE. He Loved GOD and Obeyed HIM as well, but he had 700 wives and 300 concubines that ended up turning his heart away from **GOD ALLMIGHTY**.

- <u>Adam</u> lost his intimate relationship with **GOD**, because of his wife Eve. He *esteemed his wife's word higher* than **GOD'S Command**.

*There are many others who Love GOD, but they get caught up and carried away by the *lust of their own flesh*. **HOWEVER, GOD IS A GOD OF MERCY** and if you **truly** Love HIM, HE has **MERCY** and **GRACE** that eats up all HIS Children's shortcomings. **Not to be taken for granted**, because **THE MORE GOD LOVES YOU** and HE Shows you **HE LOVES You,** the more you will express your Love for HIM by **Obeying HIM more** and fight against the flesh sin-filled nature. Live in **THE SPIRIT**!

What shall we say then? Is there unrighteousness with **GOD**? Certainly not! For HE says to Moses, "I will have Mercy on whomever I will have Mercy, and I will have Compassion on whomever I will have Compassion." So, then it is not of him/her who wills, nor of him/her who runs, but it is **of GOD** who shows Mercy **(Romans 9:14-16)**.

Lesson 6-More Sex

*We will now look at *GODLY men* who did not struggle with having sex and having sex GOD'S Way.

1. **Joseph**- *ran from* his master's wife when she grabbed him and tried to make him sex her, he still got blamed for *rape* by her and was thrown into prison.

2. **Paul**- was *too focused* on the calling and duty that **GOD** had for him to fulfill.

3. **JESUS-** The SAVIOR of The World, never committed a sin and ladies supported HIS Ministry, they were at the tomb before the disciples, after the death and RESURRECTION OF THE CHRIST.

Here are some facts about sex.

-Sex was Created BY GOD, for **married** people and **reproduction.**
-GOD created sex to happen between *a male* and *a female.*
-Homosexuality is not created by **GOD THE ALLMIGHTY** (Romans 1:16-32)
-Wanting the same sex whether you are male or female, goes against The Nature of **GOD.**
-Sex is honored by GOD only when it is done the right way, between a man and his wife.

Read James 1:12-15 & 1Corinthians 10:13

*Foot Note: For more in debt **TRUTH** on homosexuality please read Romans 1:16-32.

Lesson 7-Is Your Church Congregation Black or White

There is **no partiality** with GOD.

1. **JESUS** died for_____ (John 3:16-17).
   A. Black People
   B. White People
   C. Hebrew People
   D. All People

2. Read John 13:34-35; **JESUS** said, you will know MY Disciples by the _____ that they show.
   A. Love
   B. Money
   C. Hate
   D. None of these

Food for Thought: If you go into a predominantly black people church thugged out, (dress like what they call a thug), they will treat you with prejudice. If you stepped into a predominantly white church thugged out, just imagine how they would react. Would either congregation try to see *the person's heart* or even think that they could possibly **Love GOD and Follow CHRIST**? *Probably not*, because they need a lot more of **JESUS**. Does **GOD Our FATHER** look at the color of our skin or does HE look at us with LOVE and know our hearts? THE BIBLE Says, **LET EVERYTHING THAT HAS BREATH PRAISE THE LORD!** We are all human, so there is just one race, and that is humanity/people.

Acts 17:26- GOD has made from One Blood, Every Nation of humans, to dwell on all the face of the earth

3. According to **Philippians 2:3-4,** we are to esteem (think of others more highly) than ourselves and not only look out for our own interest but look out for the interests of others as well. Is this THE TRUTH or False? Circle one.

Quick Peek: Genesis 1:26-28, Genesis 5:1-2, Deuteronomy 10:17-18

*Why is there still segregation in the church? Is there still racism in the church? Is the church prejudice toward those who do not look like or dress like them? What do you think the Children of GOD look like to HIM? *America* has taught us how to be *prejudice* and *racist*. When you fill out certain paper work, school and job applications, etc. they all ask for your race. The options they give you to choose from **do not** include an option for **human**. Is seeing one another in color just another trick of the enemy? Yes, because it keeps us divided and not looking at each other thru the eyes of **Love**. **GOD LOVES AND REQUIRES UNITY**.

JESUS SACRIFICED HIS HUMAN LIFE FOR THE ENTIRE HUMAN RACE

Lesson 8-America

Does USA stand for <u>Under satan's Authority</u>???

But **don't worry**, satan is under **GOD THE ALLMIGHTY'S AUTHORITY**, yes he still must answer to **GOD**! **GOD IS IN COMPLETE CONTROL**.

1. America should serve **GOD** and **not** satan! (THE TRUTH or False) circle one.

2. Think about this: Could it be said that U.S.A. stands for *Under satan's Authority*?????

   BUT GOD is still in Complete Control and satan is still under **GOD THE ALL-MIGHTY'S AUTHORITY & POWER!**

3. Read Matthew 3:2 & 4:17

4. Why is America rejecting **GOD** and **HIS WAY** and embracing the devil? Is it because of all the material goods that he offers? (Read Luke 4:4-8)

Personal Note: This is not a muslim nation, buddist nation or religious nation and it sure is **not** a devil nation or a live how you want with no consequence nation, but **this nation was chosen by GOD ALL-MIGHTY to be a JESUS CHRIST Nation!**

(Order: "*The Mis -Education of America*"- by Joshua Grant coming soon!)

Lesson-9 Forgiveness

Forgiveness is Me, *letting go* of **my anger** and **my desire** to *punish* someone who has *wronged* me.

1. Read **(Matthew 18:21-22)**.

THE TRUTH or False:

2. You are Forgiven and Brought closer to **GOD THE FATHER by THE BLOOD OF JESUS**! **(Ephesians 1:7 & 2:13)**
3. **GOD LOVES** us and just wants us to Receive JESUS? **(John 3:16-17)**
4. **GOD** Forgives us, though we Rebelled against HIM? **(Daniel 9:9-11 & Romans 9:15-16)**
5. **GOD** Loves it when you keep the ten commandments (sacrifice), more than when you Love people and show Mercy? **(Matthew 9:13)**
6. Joseph **Forgave** his brothers after they became *envious* of him and sold him into slavery? **(Genesis 45:5,8)**

Did you Know???

1. **GOD** is **THE LORD** and **HE IS Good**, HE is also **Ready to FORGIVE** and has A Whole Lot of Mercy for those who call on HIM? **(Psalm 86:5)**
2. **GOD** cannot sin, Hates sin, but **FORGIVES** sin.
3. In **JESUS,** we have *Redemption* through **HIS BLOOD**, and are Forgiven for our sins thru it. **(Ephesians 1:7)**

4. If we **confess** *our sins* **to GOD**, HE is Faithful and Just to FORGIVE us our sins and HE *Cleanses* us from **ALL** unrighteousness. **(1John 1:9)**

5. If we say we have not sinned, we make **GOD** a liar and **HIS WORD** (**THE TRUTH**) is not in us. **(1John 1:10)**

6. We are to remember that we are all human, nobody is perfect and we must **FORGIVE each other**, like **CHRIST** Forgave us. **(Colossians 3:13)**

LORD HELP US ALL TO SHOW MORE MERCY AND FORGIVE ONE ANOTHER!

Lesson-10 Hidden Treasure

Read Hebrews 11:24-27.

1. *The <u>condition of **your** heart</u>* should be to have Treasure laid up in HEAVEN rather than laying up treasure on earth (chasing $$$) **THE TRUTH or False?** (See Matthew 6:19-21).
2. If you chase **GOD'S KINGDOM** AND **HIS RIGHTEOUSNESS <u>First</u>,** HE will add everything else that you need and that the world tells you to go after to your Life. **THE TRUTH or False** (Matthew 6:33)
3. Remember *EVERYTHING* belongs to **GOD**, Read 1Chronicles 29:10-14.
4. If Riches increase, please take Psalm 62:10-12 to Heart!
5. Read about this Rich man, who became even Richer in Luke 12:13-21.
6. **THE KINGDOM OF HEAVEN** is like: (see Matthew 13:44)
    A. Hidden Treasure
    B. Earth
    C. Christmas
    D. None of these

7. All that is in this world is against **GOD** and is passing away (Read 1John 2:15-17).
8. **RIGHTEOUSNESS** is more valuable than RICHES, **THE TRUTH or False** (see Proverbs 11:4)
9. For your Blessing go Read Deuteronomy 28:12-13.

Personal Note: It is Hidden Treasure, so you must go look for it in these scriptures.

Lesson-11 What is HOLINESS?

HOLINESS- is having **THE BLOOD OF JESUS** over your **LIFE and being Set apart by GOD, for GOD'S Use. GOD ALONE IS HOLY! First** Receive **JESUS**. HE then gives you The Right to become Children of GOD, believe in HIS NAME and Be **Born of GOD John 1:12-13.**

*No one is HOLY like THE LORD. (THE TRUTH or False) **Answer: (1Samuel 2:2)**

*Please Read **Revelation 15:4**.

Food For Faith: How are you living? Does the way you Live offend GOD? You can know the answer by looking in The Mirror of GOD'S WORD. You will find out that *what man is teaching* is not what GOD IS SAYING! Abraham was not even" Saved" but he *believed Every Thing that GOD said*, and GOD accounted that as Righteousness.

1. Do we receive THE SPIRIT by working The Law or by believing **GOD**?

   Answer: Galatians 3:2-9

   *But that no one is **justified** by the law in THE SIGHT OF GOD is evident, for The Just Shall Live By **Faith**! Galatians 3:11

Did You Know???

The Scripture has confined all under sin, that THE PROMISE OF GOD, by Faith in JESUS CHRIST might be Given to those who Believe. However, before FAITH came, we were kept under guard by the law, kept for The Faith, which would afterward be revealed. Therefore, the law was our tutor to bring us to CHRIST, that we might be Justified By Faith. But after Faith has come we are no longer under a tutor (Galatians 3:22-25).

FOR YOU ARE ALL **SONS OF GOD THROUGH FAITH IN CHRIST JESUS**! **(Galatians 3:26)**

Lesson 12-Holiness Comes Through GRACE

<u>GRACE-</u> is **GOD** giving us what we do not deserve. HIS daily Care, Strength, Guidance, and all other Good things. **GOD'S Promise** of **Eternal Life** with **THE LORD**.

1. There were two things that **JESUS** brought for us to have through HIM, what are they?
   A. Darkness and Confusion
   B. Grace and Truth
   C. Law and Order
   D. Money and Power (John 1:17)

2. We are justified freely by *GOD'S GRACE*, through the *redemption* that is in **CHRIST JESUS**! **The Truth or False (Romans 3:24)**

3. Did you know that **GOD'S Strength** is made Perfect in *your weakness*? (see 2Corinthians 12:9)

4. Read 2Thessalonians 2:16-17

5. Did you know that all humans are brought closer to **GOD ALLMIGHTY** by **THE BLOOD OF JESUS**? (Ephesians 2:13)

GOD does have Standards and Guidelines that we are to pattern our lives after. But just know that it is also up to GOD to show

Mercy! There is therefore now _No Condemnation_ to those who are in CHRIST JESUS, who do not Live according to the flesh but according to The Spirit.

Food for Thought: For Further Understanding and Revelation
Read Hebrews 9:18-28

Lesson 13-satan Lose GOOD News

JESUS said, "I saw satan Fall like Lighting from HEAVEN!" Luke 10:18

1. Have you received *your Authority*, that is available to you, from **GOD** according to Luke 10:19?

2. Did you know that your name is written in HEAVEN, (if you receive JESUS) and you have the right to Rejoice because of this (Luke 10:20)?

3. Did you know that **GOD** had satan kicked out of HEAVEN Read Revelation 12:7-10.

4. **We Overcome, the devil by THE BLOOD OF JESUS and The Word of Our Testimony, and we don't Love our lives in this world to death.**

   Food For FAITH: JESUS was brought forth to DESTROY the evil works of satan (1John 3:8 & Regular John 10:10-11).

   ### SALVATION (Ephesians 2:13)

   Salvation is *Freedom* from the *penalty*, *power*, and *presence* of sin. This kind of *Freedom* is from **GOD,** and is only based on **GOD'S Goodness**; not our goodness. We receive this through **Grace** and are brought near to **GOD** by THE BLOOD OF JESUS!"

5. When you hear of wars, and rumors of wars, when nation rises against nation, and kingdom against kingdom, **don't be troubled by it**!

6. There will be pestilences (fatal epidemic diseases), starvation, and many earthquakes in unique places. They will hate you and deliver you up to tribulation and kill you all because **you Live for and with JESUS THE CHRIST LORD & SAVIOR OF THE WORLD!**

7. **To see how the story ends you must Read it for yourself in Revelation 5:1-7**

JESUS PREVAILS AS THE LAMB AND THE LION!

8. For this reason, we bow our knees to **THE FATHER** OF **OUR LORD JESUS CHRIST**, WHO joins The Whole Family in HEAVEN and Earth together. We Pray that HE would grant you strength with might through *HIS SPIRIT* and that you allow **CHRIST** to dwell in your heart through Faith and be **rooted and grounded** in **LOVE**. Knowing **THE LOVE OF CHRIST** passes knowledge, and that you be filled with the Fullness of GOD. **(Ephesians 3:14-21)**

Lesson 14-JESUS

1. **Meditate** on this: **JESUS IS THE WORD OF GOD! JESUS EXISTED IN THE BEGINNING WITH GOD! GOD MADE ALL THINGS THROUGH JESUS! GOD IS JESUS!**

2. **Read** this for yourself: John 1: 1-4 & 14

3. **The Gospel of JESUS CHRIST is The Power of GOD to Salvation for Everyone that Believes,** see Romans 1:16 **(The Truth or False)**

*Did you Know: **Redemption for All Humans is in JESUS. This is done all through HIS BLOOD SACRIFICE, we have** The FORGIVENESS **of sins through GOD'S GRACE**!

4. **Reconciliation- JESUS** reconciles all humans to **GOD THE ALL-MIGHTY FATHER** (brings together rightly) Read Colossians 1:19-23 for yourself.

Perfection- The Only PERFECT One who ever lived on Earth is JESUS! Perfect Love Casts out Fear. **1 John 4:18**

5. **JESUS** is Above all Principalities and Powers (The Truth or False) **see Ephesians 1:21 & Colossians 2:10.**

6. **JESUS IS THE DOOR TO GET INTO GOD'S HOUSE!**

7. **GOD RAISED JESUS UP FROM Death, read it for yourself** Acts 2:31-36.

8. **Hope- JESUS** does not leave you Hopeless! **JESUS** gives you Hope even in a seemingly Hopeless situation so that you can keep going.

9. **YES, JESUS IS** COMING BACK **REAL SOON, please read it for yourself** Matthew 24:27-31 & 36-39 & 1Thessalonians 4:13-18 & 1Thessalonians 5:1-4.

Lesson 15-Rule in The Midst of All Your enemies

1. _Enemies_ are, anything that's against You and **Your FAITH in GOD**! (fear, sin, sickness, death and satan just to name a few).

2. Did you know that you can **Rule** Over your enemies? Rule- the _exercise of Authority_ or Control over, to be Supreme or Outstanding.

3. **Read:** Psalm 110:1-2; Psalm 25:2; Psalm 23:5

4. According to _Colossians 3:15_ What shall we let Rule in our Hearts as Followers of JESUS THE CHRIST?

5. **GOD** ruling in us makes us Rulers. For **proof** please Check out: Psalm 59:1-2, 13, 16-17 & Psalm 66:3, 7, 20.

6. Did you know you can rule _your Spirit_? When you rule _your Spirit_, you are _mightier_ than a man that takes over a city? (Proverbs 16:32). **Be slow to Anger!**

7. **Self-Control-** staying in charge of _my thoughts_, _my feelings_ and _my actions_; rather than letting them rule me. (Galatians 5:22-23)

8. **Conqueror-** a winner, an overcomer, the one who over throws or defeats, **We are More than Conquerors thru THE CHRIST JESUS!** (Romans 8:37)

9. Faith, A Clean Heart, Health, Life, and JESUS allows us to rule in the midst of our enemies. Read Psalm 23:4-6 to **Power up!**

10. **Keep PRAISING GOD THE ALLMIGHTY ABBA FATHER!** Another Guaranteed way to Rule _in the midst of_ Your Enemies!

Lesson 16-ENDURANCE

Endurance-*Continuing* to *do right* and *moving forward* during times of weariness (tired), pain, or opposition.

1. *Food for FAITH: <u>FAITH</u> *Endures (outlasts) Trials*! *Trials* and *Test* come and go but **A Strong FAITH** will face them Head-on and develop *Endurance*.

2. **Did you know...** *JESUS endured *Hostility* from sinners? Do not become weary (tired) or discouraged in your souls, we have not yet resisted to bloodshed, striving against sin **(Hebrews 12:3-4).**

   *By FAITH** Moses, *refused* to be called *the son of Pharaoh's daughter* and *chose* to suffer affliction (misery, trouble, hardship, suffering) **with GOD'S People** rather than to Enjoy the *passing pleasures of sin*. He held **the reproach** (criticism) **of CHRIST,** *Greater Riches* than The Treasures of The World!

3. Let me ask you something, "Can the sufferings and hardships of this life Compare to **GOD'S GLORY** that **shall be Revealed in us**? (Answer **Romans 8:18-19**).

4. Endure and go thru what you have to go through but if we do not Give up and continue to do good **with JESUS**, we shall receive a reward, Please **Read Hebrews 10:32-39.**

Did You Know:

5. The human that Endures temptation; when they are *approved* by **GOD**, will receive **The Crown of Life** which **THE LORD** has PROMISED to those who **LOVE** HIM (**James 1:12**).

6. **JESUS ENDURED**: Being mocked and picked on. **JESUS ENDURED**: Being betrayed by one of HIS close Followers. **JESUS ENDURED**: Being locked up and innocent. **JESUS ENDURED**: Harsh treatment by non-believers, and self-righteous, and man mad governments who refused to Acknowledge him as **LORD**. **JESUS ENDURED**: Being blasphemed against, they accused HIM of using satan's power to cast out demons. **JESUS ENDURED**: Being spit on, slapped and beat down!

7. **JESUS ENDURED**: Rejection from those whom HE suffered for. **JESUS ENDURED**: Carrying that heavy cross. **JESUS ENDURED**: The spikes being driven through HIM to hold

8. HIS Body to The Cross. **JESUS ENDURED**: Dying on the cross, death, hell, and the grave! **JESUS ENDURED**: The Journey through this life. **JESUS ENDURES**: **Being mistreated and our sins even now! THANK YOU, JESUS!**

Lesson 17-Watch Your Mouth

Watch- pay attention to the words coming out of your mouth. Are you speaking LIFE or death, Positive or negative?

1. *Did you know???* LIFE and death are in the power of your tongue??? **Read Proverbs 18:21.**

2. **Read and Meditate on Numbers chapter 12:** GOD'S People Complained against their leader whom GOD CHOSE and they Complained against GOD and had to suffer severe consequences. Watch your mouth, because **GOD is watching it**, Always!

3. So, THE LORD said to him, "WHO has made man's mouth? Or WHO makes the mute, the deaf, the seeing or the blind? Have NOT I THE LORD? Now therefore, **go, and I will be with your mouth and teach you what you shall say**." *Exodus 4:11-12*

4. For there is not a word on my tongue, But behold **O LORD YOU know** it altogether. **Read and Understand Psalm 139:1-4.**

5. Whoever *guards their mouth* **preserves** their Life, but whoever opens their lips wide shall have destruction. Whoever despises THE WORD will be destroyed, but whoever Fears THE COMMANDMENT will be rewarded Proverbs 13:3 and 13.

6. **PRAY this Verse over your Life:** Psalm 19:14.

7. **Did you know???** **It is Not what goes into the mouth of a human that defiles** (corrupts, ruin) **them, but it is what comes out of their mouth that defiles them** Matthew 15:11.

8. **Read and Meditate on Matthew 15:17-20** for more in depth understanding.

9. *The tongue* is little and **boast great things**. *The tongue* is a fire, a world of *iniquity (wickedness/ outrage)*, it defiles our whole body. Humans have tamed all kinds of animals but **No human can tame the little tongue**! The tongue is an *unruly* **evil**. **Read James 3:5-10 for more Understanding.**

10. Our tongue was **Created by GOD** to **GLORIFY HIM** and **EXALT** JESUS *OUR LORD & SAVIOR*! Remember **GOD'S WORD** gives every human **LIFE** and **COMFORT** Read Psalm 119:49-50.

Lesson 18-Tradition VS OBEDIENCE

1. **Tradition-** the *old* usual way of doing things; ways, beliefs, and customs passed down from generation to generation

2. **Obedience-** submissive to the command of authority, (stop being like goats, Behave like sheep)

*Personal Note: Stay up-to-date and tuned into what's going on so you can **COMBAT** it!

3. Did you know that you can go against/disobey GOD by keeping a *tradition*?

4. **(Please Read Matthew 15:1-3)**

5. **JESUS** said, these people draw near to **ME** with their mouth, and Honor **ME** with their lips, *but* **THEIR HEART** is far from **ME**, teaching as doctrine (as GOD'S WORD), *the commandments of men* Matthew 15:8-9.

6. Please **Read**: Mark 7:1-9 & 13 it is very important! DO NOT LAY ASIDE NOR REJECT THE COMMANDS OF GOD!

7. **JESUS** did not Teach us how to be fault finders and focus on somebody else's shortcomings for **ALL HAVE SINNED and FALL Short of GOD'S GLORY**! **JESUS** DID TEACH US *HOW TO* **LOVE** Everybody!

8. Did you know that when you continue in **THE DOCTRINE OF CHRIST**, **You have** **A** <u>RELATIONSHIP</u> **WITH THE FATHER & THE SON?** (see 2John 1:9)

"I write to you, *little children*, because **your sins** are **FORGIVEN** you for **HIS NAME'S SAKE.**

I write to you, *Fathers*, because **you have** <u>known</u> **HIM WHO is from the beginning**.

I write to you, *Young men*, because **you have OVERCOME** the wicked one!

I write to you, *Little Children*, because **you have** KNOWN **THE FATHER**.

I have written to you, *Fathers*, because **you have** <u>known</u> **HIM WHO is from the beginning.**

I have written to you, *Young men*, because **you are** <u>Strong</u>, **THE WORD OF GOD abides in you**, and **you have OVERCOME** the wicked one!

1John 2:12-14"

Lesson 19-Right vs Left Field Thinking

(Musically Speaking)

1. What kind of Music do you *like*? What kind of Music do you *listen* too? Lets look at music from **three** different **overall** perspectives:
   GOD Music
   Positive Music
   Negative Music

2. Let's start with a look into ***Negative Music:*** This music comes from the Flesh, fallen from GOD Sinful Nature, five *senses* and *understanding* without **GOD's SPIRIT**. This type of music tears the inner human and soul down. It glorifies Money, things and sin. Copy cats and fake Hollywood stars etc. are known for making this kind of music. This music is so discouraging because it leads its listeners away from THE TRUTH (JESUS). It is under the influence of satan, it is evil and it is open to all kinds of attacks from the enemy.

   Negative Music changes the world for the enemy and against **THE HOLY GOD**! It is under the influence of the devil. He influences us to use our human Gifts and Talents from GOD and for GOD, to use them for and narrow them down to money, fame, and riches. **Please** pause and **Read** Matthew 4:8-11 & Luke 4:5-8 also Matthew 6:19-21. Negative music is unrighteous; **it does not GLORIFY GOD** and leads its listeners down the road to **Destruction!**

3. We will now have a look at <u>Positive Music:</u> This music *can possibly* be Acceptable to **GOD**. This music does not tear down but it **empowers** and *inspires* its listeners. Positive music may **try to** GLORIFY GOD. This music is not too popular, but it is encouraging and strong. It may make a change **for good** but it is only under human influence. Those who make this type of music use their talents to help others and maybe to get paid.

   Positive music, if it does not decide to **follow CHRIST JESUS** it will end up being negative. **Please Read**: **Revelation 3:15-22 & Mark 8:36.**

4. Last but in no way, the least we will have a look at <u>GOD MUSIC:</u> GOD made and gave us all, our Gifts and Talents to **GLORIFY HIM**! Those who make GOD Music GLORIFY GOD and not only that, this Music is **Acceptable** to **GOD**. GOD Music Empowers and Encourages its listeners **with THE POWER of THE**

   ALLMIGHTY GOD! This music protects your soul and is **under GOD THE HOLYSPIRIT'S Control**. **GOD Music** <u>*changes the world*</u> **for CHRIST JESUS**. This music is Influenced and Inspired by **THE SPIRIT OF TRUTH**, and those who make this kind of music use their talents **for GOD** and **HIM Alone**, they will work a job for money if necessary. **GOD MUSIC** sets **GOD'S STANDARDS** in the earth. People who make this type of music usually are in a LOVING, ACTIVE Relationship with THE LORD (True Riches), and GOD Music will **last throughout ETERNITY**!

5. No One can serve two masters; for either he will hate the one and Love the other, or else either he will Be Loyal to the one and Despise the other. You cannot serve GOD and Mammon (the worldly mindset all about the $$$). Matthew 6:24.

6. Do not just honor GOD with <u>your lips</u> and have **your heart** far from HIM, for it is HE who **EMPOWERS** us to get wealth! (Deuteronomy 8:18).

*Let EVERYTHING that has Breath PRAISE THE LORD!

Lesson 20-LOVE vs Hate

LOVE- Strong Affection, Warm Attachment of a beloved person, Unselfish, Loyal, Kind, Concern for others, Devotion, Passion, **GOD IS LOVE!**

Hate- intense hostility, to express or feel extreme hostility, ill will that exists between enemies, satan is hate

These Attitudes are GOD'S ESSENCE OF LOVE
Lowliness Gentleness Longsuffering

1. **Lowliness-** being humble, not weak but meek (power under control)

2. **Gentleness-** Caring, and showing that you care for others

3. **Longsuffering-** going through hard times **peacefully** and **Godly**; showing *consideration* for others and making allowances for their shortcomings

   ***These 3 Produce UNITY, PEACE, & ENDEAVORING (Doing your Best)

   The sacrificial death of THE SON (JESUS) IS GOD'S BEST EXPRESSION OF LOVE!

4. **Please pause and read John 3:16-17** the devil a.k.a. hating satan tries so hard to Stop you from knowing this.

<u>Did you know:</u>

5. When **THE SAVIOR** wuz Crucified, HE wuz Crucified between two criminals?

6. **JESUS** and these two criminals represent everybody as *Guilty* before **GOD THE FATHER**?

7. The unique thing is that *one of the criminals* **repented** and **ACCEPTED JESUS**, the other made light of it and blasphemed (rejected/dishonored) **THE SAVIOR** WHO IS **LORD**?

8. **GOD LOVES Everybody! GOD HATES all sin and all evil?**

<u>LOVE SCRIPTURES:</u>

<u>John 14:15-18; John 15:9-19; John 13:34-35;</u>
<u>Psalm 97:10;</u>
<u>Psalm 119:104; Ecclesiastes 3:8; Proverbs 6:16-19;</u>
<u>Matthew 6:24;</u>
<u>Hebrews 13:1; 1Corinthians 13</u>

THE GREATEST GIFT IS THE LOVE OF THE ALLMIGHTY GOD! THANK YOU, JESUS!

CPSIA information can be obtained
at www.ICGtesting.com
Printed in the USA
BVOW07s1005311017
499155BV00008B/433/P

9 781545 615638